TAL
WII

By Linda Fernley

BRADWELL
BOOKS

Published by Bradwell Books

9 Orgreave Close Sheffield S13 9NP

Email: books@bradwellbooks.co.uk

British Library Cataloguing in Publication Data: a
catalogue record for this book is available from the British

1st Edition

ISBN: 9781910551332

Print: Gomer Press, Llandysul, Ceredigion SA44 4JL

Design by: Andrew Caffrey

Typeset by: Mark Titterton

Photograph Credits: Linda Fernley, Creative Commons,
others credited individually and where indicated iStock

INTRODUCTION

Wiltshire is a south-western county of England, bordered by Hampshire, Dorset, Berkshire, Somerset, Gloucestershire and Oxfordshire. It's landlocked, covers almost 1,350 square miles (3,500 sq km), and is characterised by its high downland and beautiful wide valleys.

For further factual information on the county's geography or history, or to discover which well-known places you should visit and why, may I politely invite you to head for the enormous amount of excellent tourist guide books and local history volumes – expertly researched and complied by scholars and serious travel writers – which you will surely find in any good library or bookshop.

No, it's not our purpose here to share with you the recognised facts about Wiltshire. Instead, for these Tales and Trivia books we've delighted in rummaging about to seek out the more peculiar, funny, off the wall or lesser-known tit-bits about the county's people, places, objects, customs and history. We hope that these morsels will not only

Salisbury Cathedral — iStock

add to your enjoyment of Wiltshire but will also surprise, entertain, or flabbergast you … or at least give you something to talk about when you next find yourself lost for words!

So from Harry Potter to Stonehenge, from flying monks to crop circles, and from O_2 to 007, these pages will show you a Wiltshire crying out to be explored from a different angle. You don't have to read the book sequentially from beginning to end – just dip in and out as the fancy takes you … and happy reading!

Druid's worship at Stonehenge — iStock

PUTTING WILTSHIRE ON THE MAP

On location!

Lacock Abbey was used as parts of Hogwarts School of Witchcraft and Wizardry in two **Harry Potter** films. The abbey cloisters became the school corridors through which Harry is walking when he first hears the basilisk, a giant serpent living beneath Hogwarts, in *Harry Potter and the Chamber of Secrets* (2002). Several scenes from *Harry Potter and the Half-Blood Prince* (2009) were also filmed at the abbey.

Cloisters, Lacock Abbey — iStock

In fact, arriving in the medieval village of Lacock you could be forgiven for thinking you've just entered the scene of a recent wizard battle or turned up to meet Mr Darcy for a dance at the assembly rooms! The village is a firm favourite for film and TV producers, most notably for its picturesque streets and historic cottages, untouched by modern alterations. The village's most famous appearances include the BBC's *Pride and Prejudice* and *Cranford*, and the film *The Wolfman*.

Lacock village – Past and Present Publications

Luckington Court in Chippenham, a beautiful Grade II listed building, was chosen as Longbourn, the residence of the fictional Bennet family in *Pride and Prejudice*.

When groups of visitors take tours around Luckington, the more avid fans of the period drama get into the spirit by dressing up in Regency attire and sometimes even attend balls and dinners arranged there.

The house's owner, Mrs Angela Horn, had lived at Luckington for 40 years and during the ten weeks of filming found she rather liked hosting a 70-strong film crew. 'They became like a family. I cried at the thought of them leaving. But I cheer up by reminding myself that I now have enough money to re-roof the west wing!'

Wiltshire is regarded as the '**world capital of crop circles**'. These are geometric rings in which the crop, usually corn, wheat, barley or rape, is systematically flattened into complex but often beautiful patterns. The intricate designs 'miraculously' appear overnight and can be hundreds of feet in diameter. The phenomenon originates from the 1980s in North Wiltshire, and continues to capture the imaginations of many. Even since Doug Bower and Dave Chorley revealed, in 1991, that they were behind over 200 circles around Warminster, visitors and enthusiasts from all over the world have come to the county every year to take part in crop circle tours, camps and 'night watches'. There's even a Crop Circle Access Centre, currently housed in the Wiltshire Museum in Devizes, and new circles are documented by the Wiltshire Crop Circle Study Group, who send up planes to photograph the formations.

Wiltshire crop circle
Creative Commons
Jabberocky

The new Horse on Pewsey Hill — iStock

Wiltshire's white horses

Of the 24 white horse hill figures known to have existed in Britain, 13 are or were in Wiltshire, set in the chalk downs in the centre of the county. Eight can still be seen today. Some date back around 300 years, the oldest being the **Westbury White Horse**

Westbury White Horse — iStock

on Bratton Downs. The earliest written record of the figure appears in *Further Observations on the White Horse and Other Antiquities in Berkshire*, written by the Reverend Francis Wise and published in 1742. Though the title refers to another famous horse figure, the Uffington Horse, the Reverend mentions the horse at Westbury and how he was told by locals that it had been cut in the memory of a person or people who had recently passed away, which suggests it was made in the late 17th or early 18th century. It has been re-cut twice – in 1778 by a Mr George Gee, who felt the original didn't really look much like a horse, and again in 1873, by which time it had become a bit misshapen and a special committee was put together just for the purpose.

Somewhat sadly, the high cost of maintenance led to a decision to cover over the horse's outline with concrete, which was then painted white, in the late 1950s. Other white horses can be found at Cherhill, Marlborough, Alton Barnes, Hackpen, Broad Town, Pewsey, and Devizes – the newest of all, carved in 1999 in celebration of the millennium.

This horse on **Pewsey Hill** was carved in 1937 to commemorate the Coronation of George VI. George Marples, an expert on hill carvings, was asked to come up with some designs and decided that, as it had always been so difficult to date the older horses, his design would be 'date stamped'! However, although the horse is well maintained today, the date has disappeared.

Heard about the henges?

Avebury Ring is a henge – a stone circle enclosed by a bank and ditch – built over many centuries, beginning around 2600 BC. It actually consists of three circles, the outer circle being the largest of its kind in Europe and containing the two smaller stone circles within it, known as the Northern and Southern Circles. The stones came from the Marlborough Downs, and would have required remarkable effort to move. It's thought that there were originally hundreds

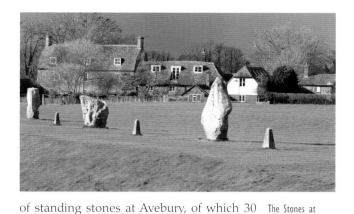

The Stones at Avebury — iStock

of standing stones at Avebury, of which 30 remain today, set in shallow holes in the chalky ground. The heaviest, known as the Swindon Stone, weighs around 65 tonnes and after 4,500 years still balances on one corner, with only a small part anchored in the ground! A great obelisk once stood in the centre of the Southern Circle at 21 feet (6.5m) high, represented today by a concrete post.

Avebury was probably used in ceremonies concerning the cycle of life and death, and still holds religious importance for modern-day pagans and druids. It seems to have fallen out of use in the Iron Age and Roman periods, but a village grew up around the henge later in Saxon times, and eventually extended into it. Much of the modern-day village of Avebury is encircled by the monument, and the High Street still follows the Saxon 'herepath' or military road. Though several stones were toppled and buried by Christians in medieval times because they were Pagan symbols, they were recovered in a 1930s project to reconstruct the site, which is open to the public today and attracts hordes of visitors, from both the UK and abroad.

The shape of the stones and circles could reveal something about their purpose. The fact that some of them are diamond-shaped and some form pillars has led to a theory that they symbolise male and female, and may have been related to fertility rites. The two small inner circles may have been for men and women to worship in separate spaces, may have served as public theatres for ceremonies, or may have represented the sun and moon.

Avebury forms part of the wider prehistoric landscape of Wiltshire, which includes such sites as Stonehenge and Silbury Hill. Stonehenge, one of the world's most iconic monuments, is another ring of ancient stones that stands on Salisbury Plain. It emerged over thousands of years, with the first part being built between 2400 and 3000 BC, when a ditch was dug with antler tools and chalk built up to make a bank. Some 500 years later, sarsen stones from the Marlborough

Stonehenge
iStock

Downs were brought to make up the inner rings, along with the smaller bluestones, all the way from the Welsh Preseli Hills.

In 2000, volunteers came from as far away as Australia to take part in an attempt to move a three-tonne stone from Wales to Stonehenge, using only the tools and methods that we know would have been available in ancient times. However, when it came to crossing choppy waters near Milford Haven, the huge stone came loose from its straps and ended up at the bottom of the Bristol Channel! The failure of the mission reignited support for the idea that the stones might have been pushed to Wiltshire by glaciers.

Silbury Hill — iStock

Like other prehistoric monuments, Stonehenge is shrouded in myth and mystery. Some argue that it was an ancient Roman temple, while others suggest it was used to calculate the dates of eclipses. It may also have been used as a place of healing and of ancestor worship. The stones are part of a landscape that's home to hundreds of burial mounds, and was almost certainly used for burials from very early times. However, the culture that created it left no records of themselves or their methods, leaving us to wonder.

In the 20th century, Stonehenge has been revived as a religious site, with New Age pagans and druids performing ceremonies there. For the most significant date in their calendar, the Summer Solstice, they're joined by thousands of visitors every year for a night of music and dancing around the stones, culminating in the sunrise over the Heel Stone on the morning of 21 June.

Silbury Hill in the Kennet valley, between Marlborough and Calne, is the tallest man-made mound in Europe and one of the largest on earth. At 130 feet (40m) high and covering over five acres, the prehistoric hill is of a similar size to the smaller Egyptian pyramids.

Crafted around 4,750 years ago from chalk and clay excavated from the local area, it would have taken an estimated 500 men working for 15 years to complete. Though its original purpose remains a mystery, it's been speculated that ancient rituals would have involved raising an elite group, perhaps a priesthood, above the heads of everyone else, to be seen for miles around, including at other monuments in the area. One legend says that the hill was made when the Devil, carrying a bag of soil with which to destroy the town of Marlborough, was stopped by priests from Avebury. In the 19th century, residents of Overton and the surrounding villages held celebrations on top of the mound every Palm Sunday. In medieval times, the round top was flattened, suggesting a defensive purpose. Whatever its origins, this stunning monument has been many things to many people over the centuries.

Wild animals and 'wifelets'

Longleat Safari and Adventure Park near Warminster, set in 9,000 acres of Wiltshire countryside, opened in 1966 as the first drive-through safari park outside Africa. It represented a breakthrough in the way animals were kept, with the visitors being the ones in a confined space (their cars) while the animals were allowed to roam freely. Today Longleat houses over 500 animals, including cheetahs, giraffes, flamingos, gorillas, and Anne the Asian Elephant.

Giraffes at Longleat — iStock

The park is situated in the grounds of Longleat House, a splendid stately home that is widely regarded as one of the finest examples of Elizabethan architecture in Britain. Once an Augustinian priory, it was partially destroyed by fire in 1567 and then rebuilt by Sir John Thynne, whose descendants would reside there for centuries to come. During World War I, Longleat was used as a temporary hospital and became the Royal School for Daughters of Officers of the Army during World War II. The house is currently home to the eccentric Lord Bath or Alexander Thynn (born Thynne), 7th Marquess of Bath. He grew up at Longleat, went on to study at Eton College and Oxford University, and began a political career. Upon inheriting the marquessate in 1992, he sat in the House of Lords as a Liberal Democrat, frequently speaking on the need for devolution for the regions of England. He lost his seat when the Labour government's House of Lords Bill excluded most of the hereditary peers.

Lord Bath is a prolific author and artist, and his elaborate murals have become an attraction at Longleat. He is well known for his colourful dress sense, apparently acquired during his time as an art student in 1950s Paris, and his unconventional love life – although married to Anna Gyarmathy since 1969, he has had relationships with around 70 other women, whom he calls 'wifelets', many of whom live in cottages on the estate.

The house is open to the public and contains a wealth of fascinating objects collected by the Thynnes over the centuries, including early medieval manuscripts, exquisite tapestries and the bloodstained waistcoat worn by King Charles I at his execution in 1649. With seven libraries containing over 40,000 books, Longleat has one of the largest private book collections in Europe.

Look out for the ghost of Louisa Carteret, wife of Thomas Thynne, 2nd Viscount Weymouth, who is said to haunt the house as the 'Green Lady'. Lady Louisa was suspected of having an affair with a young footman, who was killed when her jealous husband pushed him down the spiral staircase outside the library. Thomas hurriedly buried the young man in the cellar, telling his wife that her footman had been unexpectedly called away to attend to some family business. Louisa did not believe this story, and would stalk the corridors at night, believing her husband had locked her lover away behind one of Longleat's many doors. Taking no care to wrap up warmly, she caught a chill one night and, weakened by illness and anguish, died in childbirth in 1736 aged only 22. She has been glimpsed many times since, gliding along the corridors and knocking on doors, continuing her endless search for the footman. The corridor outside the library, where the footman met his end, is known as the Green Lady's Walk.

The famous Magna Carta

The Chapter House of Salisbury Cathedral holds one of the four existing 1215 copies of the **Magna Carta**, one of the most significant documents in English history. It was brought there by Elias of Dereham, who was present at its authorisation by King John at Runnymede and entrusted with delivering ten of the thirteen copies made. The copy at Salisbury is regarded as the finest of the four surviving originals, and still bears the marks from where King John's seal was placed. In English, the latin *magna carta* means 'great charter'. Its attempt to impose the law's limitations on a ruler is summarised in Chapter 39 of the Charter:

Magna Carta — Creative Commons engraved image by John Pine (1690–1756)

'No free man shall be taken or imprisoned, or dispossessed or outlawed or exiled or in any way ruined, nor will we go or send against him except by the lawful judgement of his peers or by the law of the land.'

CUSTOMS AND TRADITIONS

Moonrakers

The Wiltshire Moonrakers is a poem from *Wiltshire Rhymes: A Series of Poems in the Wiltshire Dialect* (1881). It tells of a folk legend in which two villagers, intent on avoiding the heavy taxes on spirits, ride up to Bristol and smuggle back a few barrels for the local pub. When their cart topples over on a bridge the barrels fall into a pond, and just as the two 'girt chaps' are retrieving their bounty, the excise men show up. The quick-thinking smugglers pretend they're trying to rake out a wheel of cheese, which is actually the moon's reflection on the water! Rolling their eyes at the simple country folk, the excise men leave them to their antics. The villagers, of course, have the last laugh, and to this day Wiltshire folk are proud to call themselves 'moonrakers' – so much so that the location of the pond in the story is hotly contested, with many villages claiming it as their own.

Wizards and druids …

The famous Marlborough College stands on the site of an old castle and it's said that **Merlin the Wizard**, from the legend of King Arthur, is buried in the school grounds under Maerl's Barrow, and that the name means 'Merlin's barrow'. The town motto is *Ubi nunc sapientis ossa Merlini* – 'Where now are the bones of wise Merlin'. However, it's since been suggested that the medieval term *marl*, 'chalky ground', may come into it, referring to the type of countryside in which the town is set!

Merlin the Wizard

Born in 1954, the eco-campaigner, neo-druid and self-declared reincarnation of King Arthur, John Timothy Rothwell changed his name by deed poll to **Arthur Uther Pendragon**. Crowned the Raised Druid King of England in 1998, he's known for his battles with English Heritage to allow legal entry to Stonehenge for the summer and winter solstice. He won, and in 2000, full public access was granted for these events. Arthur also stood for election in Salisbury in 2010 and in 2015 as an independent candidate.

A fly on your turnip!

According to a 300-year-old tradition, the newly elected MP of Salisbury serenades his or her constituents with *'The Vly be on the Turmut'* – the county's unofficial anthem – from the balcony of the White Hart Hotel.

White Hart Hotel, Salisbury — Creative Commons

Conservative party politician Robert Key (1945), Salisbury's MP from 1983 to 2010, is said to have performed this duty with gusto after every election during his 27 years of service. The song was adopted as a marching song by the 4th Battalion, TA, of the Wiltshire Regiment and is several centuries old. It's sung in Wiltshire dialect, and refers to a farmer's struggle to keep flies away from his turnips:

Twere on a jolly zummer's day, the twenty-
fust o' May,

John Scroggins took his turmut-hoe, wi' thic
he trudged away:

Now zome volks they likes haymakin', and
zome they vancies mowin'-

But of all the jobs as I likes best, gi'e I the
turmut-hoein'.

The vly, the vly,

The vly be on the turmut –

'Tis all me eye

Fer I to try

To keep vly off the turmut.

The fust place as I went to work, it were wi'
Varmer Gower:

Who vowed and swore as how I were a fust-
rate turmut-hoer;

The second place I went to work, they paid I
by the job –

But if I'd knowed a little 'afore, I'd sooner a'
bin in quod.

The vly, the vly,

The vly be on the turmut –

'Tis all me eye

Fer I to try

To keep vly off the turmut.

The last place as I went to work, they sent fer
I a-mowin',

I sent word back, I'd sooner take the zack,
than gi'e up turmut-hoein'!

Now all you jolly varmer chaps wot bides at
home so warm –

I'll now conclude my ditty wi' a-wishin' you
no harm.

The vly, the vly,

The vly be on the turmut –

'Tis all me eye

Fer I to try

To keep vly off the turmut.

If you go down to the woods today ...

There's a wealth of stories surrounding the strangely named **Sally in the Wood**, the area that lies beneath the woods of Brown's Folly near Bath. It's widely believed that 'Sally' is the ghost of a girl who died there, and now haunts the road that runs through this part of the woods. One story, published by Kathleen Wiltshire in 1984, tells that a young couple knocked down a girl when she suddenly ran from the trees onto the road. According to another version, Sally was a gypsy girl imprisoned in the nearby tower of Brown's Folly and left to waste away there. Many a late-night traveller has spotted a ghostly figure running across the road – though strangely, it's often only front-seat passengers who are able to see her.

Brown's Folly
Creative Commons
Doug Lee

Drivers have even pulled over, believing they have knocked someone down, only to find that nobody's there. Ramblers in Brown's Folly have reported seeing a gypsy girl appear among the trees, and hearing screams ringing through the woods. Katy Jordan, in *The Haunted Landscape* (2000), writes of Sally in the Wood as being a place so eerie that 'no birds sing'.

Another explanation for the name comes from the time of the Civil War, just before the Battle of Lansdown in July 1643, when the Roundheads were ambushed by the Cavaliers at Brown's Folly. Sir William Waller, who led the Roundheads, set up a makeshift bridge across the River Avon, allowing his troops to cross and lay an ambush for the enemy in 'the Woodland-wald grownd in the foote of the hill'. A fight ensued, continuing up to Monkton Farleigh and over to Batheaston. It's possible that the term 'sally' may refer to its old meaning of 'a sudden rush out from a besieged place upon the enemy', rather than to a person. Whatever the origins of the name may be, if you fancy a stroll to Brown's Folly next time you're in the area, you may have a hard time convincing anyone to come with you.

Food for thought …

Wiltshire is renowned for its **ham**. Historically, a large part of the population has kept pigs, especially in the north of the county. Swindon has been synonymous with pig farming since Saxon times, as can be read in its name: 'swine down', or 'pig hill'. The Royal Wiltshire Bacon Company in Chippenham was the main bacon business for many years, and the South Wiltshire

Museum today displays one of their bacon cookers, used for making 'Bath chaps' – the meat of a pig's cheek made into a cone shape and sliced vertically in two. The chaps were then pickled in brine, smoked or cured with salt, boiled and coated in breadcrumbs.

Wiltshire is renowned for its bacon – iStock

In Wiltshire, no part of the animal was wasted: even the trotters were boiled and eaten, and the liquid from the boiling used to set the pork in Wiltshire pork pies. The fat was stored over the year for use in a regional speciality, Lardy Cake, thought to have originated in Castle Combe. This much-loved cake traditionally consists of lard, bread dough, sugar and dried fruit – though every cook has their own variation on the recipe.

Wiltshire ham is mild and sweet-tasting, due to the traditional method of curing with bacon and molasses. Bradenham ham, a famous variety, is cured using a mixture of molasses, coriander and juniper berries and hung to mature for six months, which turns the outside black. Though it might not look appetising, Bradenham is an ever-popular ham with an intense flavour.

And what better to go in your Wiltshire ham sandwich than mustard from Tracklements, a company set up in 1970 by William Tullberg. William worked in a sausage factory, and thought it a shame that traditional methods had fallen out of use with increasing mechanisation. He also fancied something to go with his sausages, but found English mustard a little too sharp. He came across an 18th-century recipe while reading the diaries of writer and gardener John Evelyn, and, using an old coffee grinder, made the first English wholegrain mustard in his kitchen. He served portions of what he dubbed his 'Urchfont Mustard' to friends at sausage-and-mash parties he held at his home (I love the sound of these parties!). Once a local publican got a taste, all the local pubs and restaurants were after a jar of William's mustard. Today, Tracklements' hand-made mustards are enjoyed all over the world. The name comes from a word William's grandmother used to use to refer to meat accompaniments.

A Wiltshire breakfast delicacy is Bacon Fraise, which dates back to the 1600s when agricultural labourers needed a good deal of fat to get them through the tough working day. To make Bacon Fraise, simply fry bacon, cover it in a batter of eggs, cream and flour, and bake.

Devizes Pie is another pork dish that can also contain lamb, veal, tongue, offal, eggs and vegetables, and is traditionally eaten cold. It probably dates back to the 15th century, and saw a surge of popularity in the 1960s – though it has since fallen out of favour again, perhaps due to the inclusion of animal brains and entrails in the recipe.

WILTSHIRE 'NAMES'

King Athelstan (c. 895–939), the **first king of all England**, is buried somewhere in Malmesbury Abbey. Son of Edward the Elder and grandson of Alfred the Great, he was known as a brave and illustrious soldier. He was born an illegitimate child, when his mother Egwina was the King's mistress, though she later became his queen. The king was very fond of the young Athelstan; he knighted the boy at an early age, and made him the elaborate gift of a sword with a golden scabbard.

King Athelstan's tomb, Malmesbury Abbey
Creative Commons
Adrian Pingstone

Athelstan's brother Aelfweard was set to succeed to the throne on the death of the king in 924. However, he died within a fortnight of their father's death, and so Athelstan was crowned on 17 July the following year in Kingston-upon-Thames. Athelstan the Glorious, as he would become known, was a strong leader who united the Anglo-Saxons and was reputed never to have lost a battle.

A pious man, Athelstan founded several monasteries, and was known for bestowing gifts of holy relics. From the keen suitors of his sister Eadhild, Athelstan received the Lance of Charlemagne, believed to have pierced the side of Jesus, and the Sword of Constantine, whose hilt bore fragments of the cross set in crystal. He gave these to Malmesbury Abbey, of which he was particularly fond.

In Athelstan's time, Britain was ruled by several different kings and earls. The far north was the domain of the Celts, divided into the kingdoms of Alba – mostly in Scotland and led by Constantine II – and Strathclyde – today south-west Scotland, Cumbria and parts of Wales, ruled by Owen I. A group of Norse Earls, led by Olaf III Guthfrithson, King of Dublin, ruled the north of England and much of Ireland. Finally, there were Athelstan's Anglo-Saxons, who controlled most of central and south England.

After Athelstan led the Anglo-Saxons in a pre-emptive strike against the Vikings at York in 927, he was proclaimed King of the English, and the northern kings accepted his overlordship. However, King Constantine is believed to have gone back on this agreement, and formed an alliance with Olaf and Owen, who agreed that Athelstan must be stopped and so pledged to set aside their differences in order to destroy him. In 937, the Celtic–Norse army marched south to face Athelstan, who meanwhile had managed to unite the Anglo-Saxon tribes. The two forces met somewhere in north-west England and fought the Battle of Brunanburh, an event which would define the countries of England, Scotland and Wales as we know them today. Even by Middle Ages standards, this was a bloody battle; a famous poem tells of the deaths of five kings and seven earls at the hands of the Anglo-Saxons, including Constantine's son:

"Five lay still on that battlefield – young kings by swords put to sleep – and seven also of Anlaf's earls, countless of the army, of sailors and Scotsmen. There was put to flight the Northmen's chief, driven by need to the ship's prow with a little band. He shoved the ship to sea. The king disappeared on the dark flood. His own life he saved. So there also the old one came in flight to his home in the north; Constantine, that hoary-haired warrior, had no cause to exult at the meeting of swords: he was shorn of his kin, deprived of his friends on the field, bereft in the fray, and his son behind on the place of slaughter, with wounds ground to pieces, too young in battle."

Athelstan emerged victorious, and from that day England was a unified kingdom. He died in 939, at the height of his powers, after a 14-year reign. The Battle of Brunanburh still holds significance for the inhabitants of Malmesbury today, whose ancestors fought on the side of the Anglo-Saxons, and as a reward received five hides (600 acres of land) and freeman status for everyone. The Warden and Freemen of Malmesbury still own this land, and initiate new members – who must be the son of a freeman or married to the daughter of one – by having him place a silver coin into a shallow hole in the ground while reciting: '*Twig and turf I give to thee, As King Athelstan gave to me, And hope a good brother thou wilt be,*' before striking him three times across the shoulders with a hazel twig!

In his later years, James Bond author **Ian Fleming** (1908–64) was a resident of the village of Sevenhampton outside Swindon.

He and his family moved into the 16th-century manor Warneford Place in 1963, where Fleming planned to settle down and get involved in the local community, but unfortunately he died only a year later following a heart attack. He is buried in the parish church of St James.

Since Fleming's secret agent hero rose to fame, the Bond connection with Swindon has continued. In *A View to a Kill* (1985), the futuristic Renault building is the backdrop for scenes in which Bond (Roger Moore) and Sir Godfrey Tibbett (Patrick Macnee) try to stop the villain played by Christopher Walken from destroying the world, and the Motorola factory was used in *The World Is Not Enough* (1999) as an oil pumping station. Bond actor Pierce Brosnan even popped in to the nearby Plough Inn for a pint of Arkell's during filming!

'Bond ... James Bond' The Goldfinger Pub in Swindon — Creative Commons P L Chadwick

The Swindon area is now also home the only pub in the world called 'The Goldfinger' ('The Goldie' to its regulars). It was opened in 1971 by Ian Fleming's widow, Ann, and seems a fitting tribute to the creator of a character who was as fond of a tipple as Bond is – although you're more likely to find real ale and pork scratchings here than martinis, shaken not stirred!

The poet and scholar **George Herbert** (1593–1633) was rector of the parish of Fugglestone-cum-Bemerton near Wilton from 1630 until his death. He was best known for his religious poetry and popular Christian hymns, such as *Let all the World in Every Corner Sing* and *King of Glory, King of Peace*. Having been a gifted scholar, Herbert had once seemed destined for a political career, but resolved at the age of 36 to devote his life to God and the local community. He was known around Bemerton as 'Holy Mr Herbert'. The modern St Andrew's Church in Bemerton, which George restored out of his own pocket in 1630, bears a tribute to him in the form of its West Window, which depicts him in stained glass alongside Nicholas Ferrar, his publisher. A cross on the church's north wall also commemorates him, and the current church bell is still the one that would have been rung by him. Just opposite the church stands the Old Rectory, where Herbert lived in an upstairs room with a view of the church on one side and across the river to Salisbury Cathedral on the other. The Rectory receives visitors from all over the world who have been influenced by Herbert's work and come to see the place where he worshipped and spent his final days.

The architect **Sir Christopher Wren** (1632–1723) was born in the village of East Knoyle, where his father was the rector. Christopher was born in lodgings above a shop, where the family had been forced to move temporarily after a fire at the Rectory. Wren is most famous for designing buildings in London after the Great Fire of 1666 (including the beautiful St Paul's Cathedral) but he also recommended to his friend Bishop Seth Ward that the spire of Salisbury Cathedral be strengthened. The design of Farley church in Wiltshire may have been influenced by Wren because he knew both the builder and the sponsor.

Wren's magnificent St Paul's Cathedral — iStock

Vikram Seth (born in 1952) is an Indian novelist, travel writer, poet, biographer and memoirist. He lives near Salisbury in the former home of the above-mentioned George Herbert and can often be seen at literary and cultural events. His travel writing includes *From Heaven Lake: Travels Through Sinkiang and Tibet,* which won him the Thomas Cook Travel Book Award. Novels include *The Golden Gate* (1986), *A Suitable Boy* (1993) and *An Equal Music* (1999). At 1,349 pages and 591,552 words, *A Suitable Boy* is one of the longest novels ever published in a single volume in the English language!

Sir Terry Pratchett (1948–2015), best known for his *Discworld* series of comic fantasy books, lived in Broad Chalke near Salisbury with his wife Lyn and daughter Rhianna from 1993. He was the bestselling UK author of the 1990s, and received the OBE for services to literature in 1998. He could sometimes be seen in his local pub, the Queen's Head, enjoying a half pint of Badger Ale. He was fond of walking on the downs, and noted that he took inspiration from 'the mythology and folklore of the chalklands' for his 2003 novel *The Wee Free Men*, which is set on chalkland within the fictional Discworld universe. After being knighted in 2010, Pratchett decided he needed a suitable sword, and so dug 80 kilos of iron ore from a field, constructed a kiln in his garden, and forged his own. Hidden in the sword were also fragments of meteorite – perhaps a reference to the god Blind Io, a character of Pratchett's who could throw thunderbolts.

Legendary designer and photographer **Sir Cecil Beaton** (1904–80) had two homes in Wiltshire. A passion for gardening and a fondness for village life are seemingly what drew him to the county. He first visited Ashcombe House near Shaftesbury in 1930, with sculptor Stephen Tomlin and writer Edith Olivier. Of his first impressions of the Georgian manor house, he wrote: 'We inhaled sensuously the strange, haunting – and rather haunted – atmosphere of the place … It was as if I had been touched on the head by some magic wand.' It was leased to him that same year for the piffling amount of £50, on the condition that Beaton would make some improvements to the near-derelict building. This he did, with the help of Austrian architect Michael Rosenauer, constructing a passageway through the house to connect the front and back sections, and elongating the windows. Plumbing and electricity were installed and a front door surround was designed by artist Rex Whistler, which included a pineapple made of Bath stone. During his time there, Sir Cecil entertained many great actors and artists of the era such as Tallulah Bankhead, Ruth Ford and Lord Berners, and artists such as Salvador Dali and Christian Bérard painted murals on the walls. In 1948, Cecil designed a fabric and named it the Ashcombe Stripe, after his beloved home. He recounted his life at Ashcombe in a book titled *Ashcombe: The Story of a Fifteen-Year Lease* (1949). Needless to say, he was heartbroken when the lease expired in 1945, upon which he moved to

Reddish House, home of Cecil Beaton Creative Commons Fryfilm2000

Reddish House in Broad Chalke. He again worked at transforming the house, even repurposing cages that had once been used for cockfighting into wardrobes for storing his Oscar-winning costumes for *My Fair Lady*. He lived at Reddish until his death at the age of 76, and is buried in the village churchyard.

Ashcombe House has also been home to British director **Guy Ritchie** (1968), best known for his crime comedy films including *Lock, Stock and Two Smoking Barrels* (1998) and *Snatch* (2000). He moved to Ashcombe in 2001 with his then wife, international pop star **Madonna**. The 'Queen of Pop' infamously fell from a horse while riding at Ashcombe on her 47th birthday. Though the couple have now divorced, Ritchie still lives at Ashcombe, and in fact was recently remarried there (July 2015), to model Jacqui Ainsley.

Singer **Rosemary Squires**, MBE (born in 1928) was brought up in Salisbury. Known as 'the Queen of Jingles', she was made famous by singing for early television ads

– particularly the 'Hands that Do Dishes' theme for Fairy Liquid, which ran for over four decades. She started off with singing, guitar and piano lessons at St Edmund's Girls' School, and made her first broadcast on the BBC's *Children's Hour* aged just 12. During the 1940s, she flourished as a Big Band and cabaret singer, honing her talents at local gigs around her home city and entertaining troops at UK and US army bases. With her distinctive West Country burr, she went on to top the bill at the London Palladium, appeared at several gala and royal events, and worked with such stars as Sammy Davis Jr, Danny Kaye and Cliff Richard. However, she never favoured the limelight, and was known to prefer going home for a cup of tea after a show rather than attending showbiz parties. Rosemary was awarded the MBE in 2004 for services to music and received the British Music Hall Society's Lifetime Achievement Award in 2012.

Film star **Diana Dors** was born Diana Mary Fluck in Swindon in 1931. She loved film from a young age, taking her first trip to the cinema with her mother, Mary, at age three. She was educated at Selwood House, a small private school run by puritanical sisters Miss Daisy and Miss Ruth, and, to their exasperation, spent most of her time doodling the names of film stars in the margins of her exercise book. In 1944, as D-Day approached and thousands of Americans entered Britain, Diana was thrilled at the prospect of meeting one for the first time. Sure enough, the Flucks offered their spare bedroom to several American guests, whom Diana bewildered and amused with questions about the lives of her favourite Hollywood stars.

At 12, she already knew how to apply make-up and wore her golden hair long, causing quite a stir as she walked around town. Accompanied by Mary, she started attending dances and parties every Sunday, where she mingled with Americans. When the end of the war sent them all back across the Atlantic, she longed more than ever to join them.

Diana won her first beauty contest while on holiday in Weston, and appeared in the Swindon newspaper wearing a white and scarlet swimsuit. This was how she landed her first modelling job, posing for an art professor at an American college that had opened nearby, earning one guinea an hour for her trouble. She was soon invited to take part in theatre productions at the college, playing the lead in Alberto Casella's *Death Takes a Holiday* (1934), and also started singing on the college radio station. At 14, she was finally allowed to leave the school that so bored her and was sent to the London Academy of Music and Drama as the youngest full-time student the academy had ever had. While at LAMDA, she landed her first walk-on film role in *The Shop at Sly Corner* (1947). It was suggested that she change her slightly awkward surname; as Diana put it, 'I suppose they were afraid that if my real name, Diana Fluck, was in lights and one of the lights blew …' She took her grandmother's maiden name at her mother's suggestion, who thought that two names beginning with the same letter sounded bold and appealing for a film star!

Diana Dors with Phil Silvers, 1958
Creative Commons

With a few more small parts in films, at 15 she was bringing back to Swindon more money than her father was earning. By the mid-50s, she had come into her own and was known as 'the English Marilyn Monroe'. She finally made it to New York in 1956, starring in *The Unholy Wife* the following year and many more pictures thereafter. She returned to her hometown in 1978 for a book signing, welcomed by fans and old friends. The 'Siren of Swindon' died in 1984 and is buried in Sunningdale, Berkshire.

The current Dean of Salisbury Cathedral, **The Very Reverend June Osborne**, is the first woman ever to serve as Dean at an English medieval cathedral and is the Church of England's most senior woman priest. She was born in Manchester in 1953 and studied social sciences at Manchester University, before training for the Church's ministry at St John's College, Nottingham and Wycliffe Hall, Oxford. She became Deaconess of Birmingham's St-Martin-in-the-Bullring in 1980, and later moved to the Old Ford parishes in East London. She was one of the original 1,500 women to be ordained in 1994. She moved to Salisbury in

1995 as Canon Treasurer of the cathedral, and was appointed the 80th Dean of Salisbury in 2004. June is a champion of diversity in the church, and a passionate campaigner on the issues of equality and poverty. She has made many visits to the Sudan and has worked with the country's Episcopal Church on health and education. She is also a lifelong Manchester City fan!

Inside Salisbury Cathedral — iStock

Author and Nobel Laureate **William Golding** (1911–93) grew up in Marlborough, which he renamed 'Stilbourne' for the setting of his novel *The Pyramid* (1967). A teaching post at Bishop Wordsworth's School in Salisbury later in life coincided with his writing of *Lord of the Flies* (1954), where

his adolescent male pupils presumably acted as inspiration for the reckless schoolboys of the disturbing tale. After living for some years in Salisbury, Golding moved to Bowerchalke in 1958, where he is now buried in the village churchyard.

William Golding plaque
Creative Commons
Peter Denton

The actor **Christopher Biggins** was born in 1948 in Lancashire and grew up in Salisbury. Christopher's father Bill was well known around the town, and ran a second-hand car business, Middleton Motors, as well as antique shops in Castle Street, Pennyfarthing Street and Winchester Street. His mother worked in local hotels and bars. A flamboyant dresser from early on, Christopher remembers he insisted on wearing a full-length blue kaftan when going out shopping with his mother. 'Sleepy old Salisbury in the early sixties had hardly ever seen the like before,' he recalls.

Christopher took part in local drama groups and was given the lead role in Moliere's *Le Médecin malgré lui* at the Salisbury Playhouse at 17. He soon signed a contract as an assistant stage manager, earning £2 a week. The following year, he was accepted into Bristol's Old Vic Theatre School, where he became great friends with the actor Jeremy Irons. He later joined the Royal Shakespeare Company, and had his first TV role as Lukewarm in the sitcom *Porridge* during the 1970s alongside Ronnie Barker. In the 1980s, he co-hosted the Saturday night show *Surprise, Surprise* with Cilla Black. He continues to star in pantomime, and is perhaps best known for his role as pantomime dame Window Twankey in *Aladdin*.

One of Christopher's favourite roles was the vicar Osborne Whitworth in the immensely popular period drama series *Poldark*. First broadcast in 1975, the series was remade and broadcast in March 2015, and filmed partly in Christopher's home county, with the town of Corsham acting as 18th-century Truro.

Great English portrait painter **Sir Thomas Lawrence** PRA FRS (1769–1830) was born in Bristol, and moved to Wiltshire in 1773. He began drawing while living in Devizes, where his father ran the Black Bear Inn. Travellers on the road from London to Bath would frequently stop in search of a meal and a warm bed, and the aspiring young painter entertained the inn's guests with poetry readings and little exhibitions of his drawings. By the age of ten, he was being hailed as a prodigy. When the family moved to Bath, he began working in pastels, and moved on to oils when he went to live in London in 1786. There, he studied briefly at the Royal Academy schools, where he became known as a charming and uncommonly gifted young man.

Thomas was a public-spirited sort of lad, and once helped travellers at his own expense by erecting signal posts across Salisbury Plain at half-mile intervals, with the mileage to Devizes and to Salisbury carved into each side. When an infamous highwayman was terrorising the neighbourhood, Thomas sent out a party of horsemen to bring him to justice, although they never caught the robber.

Thomas became known for his 'society' paintings, depicting royalty, great diplomats and famous generals – even Pope Pius VII. He was summoned to paint Queen Charlotte at Windsor in 1789, and produced what is now considered one of the great masterpieces of the time. He was renowned for his ability to portray his sitters' moods on canvas. His success soon attracted the attention of the Prince Regent, an influential patron of art and architecture at the time, and he was knighted in 1815. Thomas was sent to the Continent several years later to paint the allied military leaders, whom he depicted in elegant full-dress portraits. The 24 canvases he produced now hang in Windsor Castle. Today, he is widely regarded as the leading British portrait painter of the early 19th century.

Thomas Lawrence self-portrait, 1788 Creative Commons

A servant at the White Lion Inn, **Hannah Twynnoy** (c. 1670–1703), had the misfortune of being the first known person in Britain to be killed by a tiger. She had very unwisely been teasing the creature, which belonged to a travelling menagerie that had arrived at the inn. The tiger got its own back when it somehow managed to catch hold of her gown and tore her to pieces. A memorial stone to her can be found in Malmesbury Abbey Churchyard, which reads: 'In bloom of life, She's snatched from hence, She had not room to make defence; For Tyger fierce, took life away, And here she lies, In a bed of clay, Until the Resurrection Day'.

Michael Crawford was born Michael Patrick Dumbell Smith in Salisbury in 1942. The comedy actor became famous playing the hapless Frank Spencer in the television series *Some Mothers Do 'Ave 'Em*. He's also a singer and has starred in musicals such as *Billy* and won an Olivier Award for his performance of the Phantom in Andrew Lloyd Webber's *Phantom of the Opera*. He received an OBE in 1988.

Actor **Joseph Fiennes** (born in 1970) is the youngest of six siblings. He was born in Salisbury and went to Swan School for Boys (now Leehurst Swan School). At 11, he continued his studies at Bishop Wordsworth's School. Film roles include William Shakespeare in *Shakespeare in Love* (1998) and Martin Luther in *Luther* (2003).

Born in Swindon in 1982, **Billie Piper** started her career as a pop singer, later turning to acting. She was the youngest ever artist to debut at number one in the UK singles chart which she achieved with '*Because We Want To*'. Her most famous acting role is as Rose Tyler in *Doctor Who*. She was married for six years to DJ Chris Evans, and in 2007 married actor Laurence Fox.

MISCELLANEOUS

Blind faith!

Eilmer, a Benedictine monk of Malmesbury Abbey, attempted man's first recorded flight when he jumped from the Abbey tower in 1010 with 'wings' strapped to his arms and legs. He reportedly glided 600 feet, before spiralling back to earth and breaking his legs. Having made a full recovery, the intrepid monk was ready to try again with a few tweaks to his design, but his Abbot forbade him. A kite festival and other flight-related celebrations were held in 2010 to mark 1,000 years since Eilmer embarked on his short-lived voyage!

© Tim O'Brien

Say cheese!

The **world's oldest surviving photograph** was taken at Lacock Abbey in 1835 by William Fox Talbot. It is actually a photographic negative, no bigger than a postage stamp, depicting the oriel window in the South Gallery of the Abbey. Fox Talbot's work laid the foundations of modern photography, although he could never have foreseen that the cloisters of his old home would one day serve as the classrooms of Hogwarts in the Harry Potter films! The ambitious Talbot

Fox Talbot (John Moffat, 1864) — Creative Commons

continued his experiments and went on to discover, in 1840, the basic positive-negative principle for recording photographs. The original negative is held at the National Media Museum in Bradford.

Identity crisis?

Many people in Wiltshire no longer use words that were once commonplace throughout the county. An obvious change is the way many town and village names have been spelt differently through the ages – a good example being **Urchfont**. It's said that over the last 400 years of its recorded history the village's name has been spelt 111 different ways and probably had even more derivations before we first picked up a quill and started scribbling!

The *Urch* part of the name is said by some to originate from an old dialect word for deer, *erche*, while the *font* refers to a spring. Even in the 1930s, the village was Erchfont – and it's this spelling that can still be seen today on the plaque outside the village hall. Some other spellings include: in 1303 – Archefontte; 1334 – Icheffont; 1377 – Lerchesfonte; 1428 – Orchffunte; 1572 –

Vrshaunt; 1605 – Earchfount; and 1695 – Ushant. You can read the complete list by reading the village's local history pamphlet, *Urchfont – By Any Other Name*! Incidentally, the village is also home to a quite confusing, if amusing, road sign!

Up, down, turn around! — Creative Commons

Tick, tock ...

Salisbury Cathedral houses what is widely believed to be the **world's oldest working clock**, made of hand-wrought iron and dating from about 1386.

It has neither hands nor dials, but is designed only to strike a bell once an hour to call parishioners to service, using a system of weights and pulleys. The clock was originally housed in a separate tower, where it worked until 1884. When a new clock was installed, the old clock fell into obscurity, until it was rediscovered in 1929 and put out on display to the public. Not until 1956 was it fully restored by John Smith and Co. of Derby, and is now to be found in the aisle at the Cathedral, with nearly all of its original parts, still going strong.

All Saints Church in Westbury, built in the 14th century, is known for its **faceless clock**. Made by a local blacksmith in 1604, the clock still strikes the hours and quarter-hours and has to be wound daily. A dispute arose in 2012 when two newcomers to the village complained about the church bell ringing through the night, and insisted that the faceless clock be stopped from sounding between 11pm and 7am. The chimes were on an automated system, but a method was found of adjusting the mechanism so they would only sound during the daytime – up until then, they had rung out at all hours of the day for 100 years. For some reason, the villagers have since withdrawn their complaint, and the hourly bell now strikes through the night once more!

Small is beautiful!

Bremilham Church in Malmesbury is **the smallest 'in service' church in Britain**, measuring a tiny 13 feet by 11 feet (4 x 3.5m)! A local farmer had used it to store turkeys up until the Collins family bought the neighbouring farm and had the building consecrated. Since then, the tiny church has seen numerous christenings and burials, although a wedding might be pushing it. Inside is a single pew, seating four people, and standing room for six. Its annual service, needless to say, is held outside!

Bremilham Church
Creative Commons
White-Socks

Lady O'Looney!

A magazine published by **Charles Dickens** in the 1850s, *Household Words*, popularised an epitaph that he attributed to the Wiltshire village of Pewsey. It still turns up in anthologies of epitaphs today – you can see why:

Here lies the body of Lady O'Looney, Great Niece of Burke. Commonly called the sublime. She was bland, passionate and deeply religious, also she painted in water colours and sent several pictures to the Exhibition. She was first cousin of Lady Jones, and of such is the Kingdom of Heaven.

The Rector of Pewsey at the time, Thomas Ravenshaw, was inspired to research the subject of epitaphs and in 1878 published his own collection, *Antiente Epitaphes*, a copy of which resides at the Wiltshire Archaeological Society at Devizes. In an appendix he laid to rest the ghost of Lady O'Looney, who had never been in Pewsey at all!

The original O_2

The chemist and philosopher **Joseph Priestley** (1733–1804) discovered oxygen at Bowood House near Calne on 1 August 1774. He worked for the Earl of Shelburne as a librarian for the estate and as a tutor to his sons, and was given a room there which he used as a laboratory. In a series of experiments, using the sun's rays focused through a magnifying glass to heat mercury oxide, Priestley observed that a gas was produced that made a candle burn 'with an amazing strength of flame; and a bit of red hot wood crackled and burned with a prodigious rapidity'. Though oxygen had been produced by various chemists previously, Priestley was the first to recognise it as a distinct element.

Bowood House was the seat of the Marquess of Lansdowne and its **Capability Brown** designed gardens boast the largest area of mown lawn in England!

Bowood House — iStock

The Beast of Trowbridge

A history of local sightings of strange creatures has led to the belief that **big cats** might prowl the Wiltshire countryside. Around a thousand sightings of big cats are reported every year in the UK, and are becoming especially common in the south-west of England. Wiltshire in particular has been a hot spot for sightings of a feline creature, too big to be a domestic cat and unlike a badger, fox, or any other local wildlife.

Among the most notorious are the **Minety Monster**, believed to be behind a series of sheep killings in Minety in 2002, and the **Beast of Trowbridge**, spotted in various places around the county and described as resembling a puma or panther. The latest sighting of the Beast was reported in 2013 by a local couple, who captured footage of what appears to be a large black cat while walking in Murhill Woods in Trowbridge.

Big cats were once a common feature of private zoos and menageries, and it's believed that when the Dangerous Animals Act of 1976 placed strict restrictions on the ownership of exotic species, the animals' owners were forced to release them into the wild. As a rural county, bordering other rural counties of Somerset, Dorset and Hampshire, Wiltshire would certainly provide lots of places for wild cats to lurk.

Frank Tunbridge of Gloucestershire, who has been investigating sightings in the West Country for years (and even runs a big cat hotline), believes that Wiltshire's feline population consists of puma, lynx and a small type of black panther, as well as hybrid cats which have adapted to the environment over the last few decades. He says the animals could easily sustain themselves on woodland creatures such as rabbits, hares and pheasants. However, the scientific community remains unconvinced, arguing that a colony of large predators in a small country like ours would produce much more evidence. The official conclusion from a government report published in March 2010 is that big cats do not roam Britain. Perhaps you'll have to take a walk around the Wiltshire countryside and decide for yourself – but be prepared to make a run for it; those panthers are pretty fast!

On the run ...

On 6 October 1651 a party of riders, including a tall, dark stranger, stopped at the George

Inn at Mere for refreshment. The disguised stranger was Charles Stuart, the future King of England, on the run after his army's defeat at the Battle of Worcester. The Victorian novelist Harrison Ainsworth dramatised this event in his novel *Boscobel*

The George Inn
Creative Commons
Maigheach-gheal

or, the Royal Oak, which tells the story of Charles's flight. The whole of Chapter 22 is set in the inn and is entitled 'How they

Charles II — iStock

dined at the George at Mere, and how the host related his dream'.

The Inn was built in 1580 and renamed The Talbot through the 19th century until recently, from the crest of the Grove family who owned it. In a dining room adjacent to the main bar is a portrait of Charles II together with a framed text detailing the king's visit. It seems likely that Ainsworth visited Mere while researching the book as he includes these observations: 'While riding out of Mere, they gazed at the fine old church with its lofty tower, at the ancient market-house, and at the lofty mound on which were some vestiges of a castle, built in the reign of Henry III.'

BOOK ENDS

Here are some more random, but brief, facts about Wiltshire that I believe warrant a mention – mainly trivia but some are tales!

1. In the churchyard at Alvediston is the grave of Anthony Eden, first Earl of Avon (1897–1977), the British Prime Minister brought down by the Suez crisis of 1956.

2. South of Malborough is Martinsell Hill, the favourite viewpoint of the Old Marlburian art historian and Stalinist spy Anthony Blunt (1907–83). His ashes were scattered on the hillside there.

3. Old Sarum is the site of the original city of Salisbury; it was founded in the Iron Age and occupied until the 16th century. Romans, Saxons and Normans have all left their mark. Part of the Domesday Book was written here, and on its completion it was to Sarum that King William I summoned all the

landholders in England to swear their oath of allegiance. The international best seller *Sarum* by Edward Rutherford is largely based in the Salisbury area and Old Sarum.

4. Housed in the Crofton Pumping Station near Great Bedwyn is the oldest working steam-driven beam engine in the world, made by Boulton and Watt in 1812. It's still used for its original purpose of pumping water up to the summit level of the Kennet and Avon Canal.

5. Devizes boasts the longest flight of locks on Britain's waterways. The 29-lock stretch on two miles of the Kennet and Avon Canal climbs 230 foot high Caen Hill, and was understandably the last part of that project to be completed. It takes an experienced user a good five hours to pass through the system designed by the great canal engineer John Rennie.

6. The largest Chinese restaurant in the UK is The Pagoda Palace in Swindon!

The flight of 16 locks on the Kennet and Avon Canal
Creative Commons Roy Gray

7. The Britpop band Oasis took their name from an Inspiral Carpets tour poster in Noel and Liam Gallagher's bedroom; one of the venues was the Oasis Leisure Centre in Swindon.

Marlborough's magnificent Victorian Town Hall at the top of High Street — iStock

8. Marlborough vies with Stockton-on-Tees and Appleby for the widest high street in England.

9. Founding father of British political philosophy Thomas Hobbes, whose most famous work *Leviathan* is still required reading for students, was born in 1588 in Malmesbury.

10. Malmesbury claims to be the oldest borough in England with a charter being given by Alfred the Great in 880. But there's little documentary evidence of any charter, and even suggestions of later forgery. Historians believe the legend can be traced back to a book written in 1951. But the claim to be the oldest continually inhabited town could be true. It started life around 800 BC as an Iron Age Fort.

11. Malmesbury also played a vital part in one of the most important developments of the Second World War – radar. EKCO – Eric Kirkham Cole Limited, a British electronics company – set up a secret factory at Cowbridge House where even the workers had no idea what they were making.

12. The small Wiltshire town of Wilton is the home of high-quality carpets that are renowned worldwide.

13. The singer Sting, who came to prominence with his band The Police in the 1970s, owns an Elizabethan manor house set in 50 acres of a country estate in the picturesque Woodford Valley, near Salisbury.

14. **Sir Isaac Pitman,** the inventor of the most widely used form of shorthand, was born in Trowbridge in 1813 in a small court of houses called Naish's Yard, off the west side of Hill Street.

15. The Cathedral Close at Salisbury is the largest in Britain and is flanked with beautiful houses, some owned by famous people and open to the public.

16. **George Haden** (1788–1856) was one of Trowbridge's most prolific and successful industrial inventors. His greatest achievement related to the heating and ventilation of buildings. In 1826 at the request of King George IV he installed the heating system at Windsor Castle. He then went on to install heating systems in Wilton House, the Houses of Parliament and the British Museum reading room.

Other books in the Bradwell Books Tales & Trivia series

Available Now

Dorset Tales & Trivia

Hampshire Tales & Trivia

Somerset Tales & Trivia

Other titles for these counties include

Hampshire

Hampshire Dialect

Bradwell's Eclectica Hampshire

Bradwell's Eclectica Southampton

Hampshire Ghost Stories

Hampshire Wit & Humour

Walks for all Ages Hampshire *out in 2016*

Legends & Folklore Hampshire *out 2016*

Dorset

Walks for all Ages Dorset

Dorset Ghost Stories

Dorset Wit & Humour

Dorset Dialect

Legends & Folklore Dorset *out 2016*

Wiltshire

Wiltshire Dialect

Wiltshire Ghost Stories

Wiltshire Legends & Folklore

Walks for all Ages Wiltshire

Wiltshire Wit & Humour

Somerset

Somerset Dialect

Somerset Ghost Stories

Somerset Wit & Humour

Walks for all Ages Somerset

Walks for all Ages Exmoor

Legends & Folklore Somerset *out 2016*

For more details of these books
and other books you may be
interested in,visit
www.bradwellbooks.com

BIBLIOGRAPHY

Keith Burge & Tom Mills, *Marnin' Moonrakers!*, Countryside Books, 2008

John Chandler, *Small Talk in Wiltshire*, Ex Libris Press, 1992

Christopher Winn, *I Never Knew That About England*, Random House Group, 2008

Websites accessed June and July 2015

www.information-britain.co.uk/didyouknow.php?town=devizes&county=2

www.insidewiltshire.co.uk/about-wiltshire/notable-people/

www.athelstanmuseum.org.uk/governance_warden_freemen.html

en.wikipedia.org/wiki/Battle_of_Brunanburh

www.bbc.co.uk/history/historic_figures/athelstan.shtml

www.georgeherbert.org.uk/

www.theguardian.com/books/gallery/2015/mar/12/terry-pratchett-a-life-in-pictures

www.bbc.co.uk/wiltshire/going_out/theatre/pratchett.shtml

www.economist.com/news/obituary/21647261-sir-terry-pratchett-creator-discworld-universe-died-march-12th-aged-66-gods-and en.wikipedia.org/wiki/Ashcombe_House,_Wiltshire

en.wikipedia.org/wiki/Reddish_House

www.westerndailypress.co.uk/Madonna-felt-incarcerated-living-Guy-Ritchie/story-26152449-detail/story.html

www.rosemarysquires.co.uk/biography.htm |

www.dianadors.co.uk/

www.bbc.co.uk/wiltshire/content/articles/2005/11/15/pwaod_dors_feature.shtml

www.salisbury.anglican.org/whos-who/cathedral/the-dean-of-salisbury

www.dailymail.co.uk/tvshowbiz/article-1050839/Frank-Sinatra-Queen-Christopher-Biggins.html

www.telegraph.co.uk/culture/tvandradio/11071952/Historic-Poldark-film-location-in-Wiltshire-town-blighted-by-unnecessary-road-signs.html

www.wiltshire-opc.org.uk/Items/Devizes/Devizes%20-%20Sir%20Thomas%20Lawrence.pdf

www.devizesheritage.org.uk/lawrence_bear_inn.html

www.twilightshadowsparanormal.co.uk/sallyinthewoods.html

www.wshc.eu/blog/item/sally-in-the-wood.html

www.wshc.eu/blog/item/wiltshire-s-wild-cats.html

www.dailymail.co.uk/news/article-1282333/Leopards-big-cats-ARE-loose-Britain--just-dont-tell-soul.html

www.wiltshirewhitehorses.org.uk/westbury.html

www.visitwiltshire.co.uk/explore/the-great-outdoors/white-horses

www.westerndailypress.co.uk/Amicable-agreement-church-clock-chimes-villagers/story-17485733-detail/story.html

en.wikipedia.org/wiki/Alexander_Thynn,_7th_Marquess_of_Bath
en.wikipedia.org/wiki/Longleat

www.hha.org.uk/Property/1062/Longleat-House

www.longleat.co.uk/explore/longleat-house myths.e2bn.org/mythsandlegends/textonly1853-the-green-lady-of-longleat-house.html

en.wikipedia.org/wiki/Lacock_Abbey

www.nationaltrust.org.uk/lacock/things-to-see-and-do/lacock-village/

www.timetravel-britain.com/articles/taste/taste08.shtml

www.insidewiltshire.co.uk/food-and-drink/

www.telegraph.co.uk/foodanddrink/recipes/8281603/Tracklements-Mustard-Going-against-the-grain.html